Overrepresented

Indigenous Women as Profit Makers for the
Canadian Judicial System

ANNETTE L. VERMETTE

◆ FriesenPress

One Printers Way
Altona, MB R0G 0B0
Canada

www.friesenpress.com

ISBN
978-1-03-917192-3 (Hardcover)
978-1-03-917191-6 (Paperback)
978-1-03-917193-0 (eBook)

1. POLITICAL SCIENCE, COLONIALISM & POST-COLONIALISM

Distributed to the trade by The Ingram Book Company

"Social worker Annette L. Vermette's social science book *Overrepresented* discusses the disempowerment of Indigenous women in the Canadian justice system. The book reveals that the incarceration of Indigenous women in Canada skyrocketed by 90 percent during the 2010s; in the 2020s, Indigenous women make up over 50 percent of the total incarcerated population. And it notes that Indigenous women in Canada are also affixed with damaging stereotypes—designations that are often used as justifications for state charges that are further informed by colonial practices, including assimilation and coercion. The justice system, the book says, must be reconstructed to address these inequalities...The sobering social science book *Overrepresented* shares potent information about Canada's legal and cultural oppression of Indigenous people."

—*Foreword* Clarion Reviews

Table of Contents

Acknowledgements

Of all people, my children have seen the tireless work I have done and continue to do for the good of others. Their own perseverance and dedication is my pride and joy. To my husband, Byron, who recognized my passion for writing before I could put it into words.

Preamble

All truths are subjective, thus, the suppositions expressed in this book are subjective, based on the author's senses, perceptions, and professional observations. Therefore, the statements reflected therein are subjective. This is my truth.

Introduction

THE OBJECTIVE OF THIS PROJECT is to explore profit gains within prison-related employment sectors as a possible motivator to substantiate and perpetuate imprisonment of Indigenous women in Canada. The reported costs by the Parliamentary Budget Officer (PBO) in 2018, and other sources in this research, differ, as do the individual reported costs per woman for their incarceration in Canada. This statement is intended to clarify that each reporter (author or researcher) reports different totals. For example, one may include provincial and federal incarcerations, and another may only report federal, but this is not made clear. Some sources report the totals from PBO (as published), but Kim Pate, Parliamentary officer, states another total. I suspect this occurs because the additional costs are either not reported in the PBO or they are tabulated in a budget that does not get published. This leaves a reader unaware of the true costs.

In this research, the methods by which the judiciary and the state may forecast the monetary allocations for incarceration—as a means of satisfying the industries that supply the prison system—will be elaborated. Many employment sectors (e.g. enhanced security for solitary confinement; and various suppliers) benefit from the allocations of incarceration, and many jobs would be adversely affected should the industry of incarceration decline. My curiosity is piqued when I consider the increase in the cost of living in Canada on a yearly basis, as well as the wage increases for various employment sectors; these costs could be satisfied by the predictability of increased rates of incarceration.

From this financial platform, I critically analyze whether the money could be allocated otherwise to programming and community-based justice centres with the skills and impetus to address cycles of recidivism and satisfy culturally based healing initiatives.

To summarize, the business of crime costs society as a whole, but if the employment sectors within the current framework of criminalization sufficiently benefit, there may not be an incentive to change the judiciary's, or the state's, methods of criminalizing Indigenous women.

Chapter 1

HAS CANADIAN SOCIETY BECOME ACCEPTING of an approach of over-incarceration? Is legislature professing to be appeasing society's concerns about safety and punishment, while leaving the world of politics, law, and the state to build their own agenda and political platform? Historically, the removal of children from their families to relocate them in residential schools was instigated by a societal concern about safety, amongst other reasons. Indigenous children did not obtain their education in the same manner as other children; this was a concern that was voiced by society. The punishment, which was supported by such citizens and communities, was the new method of education. The punishment also included abuse in many forms, which is elaborated in many literatures.

In modern times, society's safety concerns surround the homeless encampments in urban centres. These concerns have aroused my curiosity regarding the expectations put on the judiciary when it comes to sentencing. In this book, I explore how colonialism aims to remove the power of choice—in essence, freedom—from women. The ways in which residential schools in Canada aimed to eliminate choice, freedom, and culture have been well documented over the last decade. The removal of Indigenous women from their communities follows this same principle. Incarceration may have become the new method of disempowering Indigenous communities, women in particular.

Considering the reported monetary tabulations and the statistics available to date, the information can be confusing. The current statistics indicate that the frequency and severity of crime in Canada have been declining; however, the criminalization of Indigenous women is on the rise. It appears to me that some systems are insistent that the beds within prisons remain filled at all costs. Is it industry, politics, government, society, or a combination of systems that insist on keeping the prisons full?

I have chosen the demographic of Indigenous women, as opposed to other populations, because this group is the fastest rising in comparison with men, Indigenous men, and non-Indigenous women. On June 10, 2019, Mark Blackburn reported for National News in an article entitled "'It's disappointing': corrections maintain status quo as a number of Indigenous women tops 40% of the prison population." He reported that "the federal inmate population has increased by 1.2%, while the Indigenous population in federal prison has increased by 52.1%." Since 2010, the female inmate population has increased 34.8%, while the Indigenous women inmate population has increased from 32.1 to 41.4% (Justice Canada March 2018). The Canadian Association of Elizabeth Fry Societies reports that 50% of all incarcerated women in Canada are Indigenous (2021) which represents 25% more than Vicky Chartrand reported in 2018. Their statement mirrors Justice Safety Canada in explaining that the incarceration represents a 90% increase in the last decade (Public Safety Canada).

In my research, I looked for possible reasons for increases for this specific population. A piece of data that particularly sparked my interest was found in an article entitled "Broken System: Why is a quarter of Canada's prison population Indigenous," written by Vicki Chartrand, Associate Professor at Bishop's University (2018). She quotes the report of The Parliamentary Budget Officer in 2018, specifying that the cost to incarcerate one woman per year is upwards of $343,810. However, Kim Pate, Independent Senator for Ontario in the Territory of the Algonquin Anishinabeg, states that "over $600,000 per year per woman for maximum security and special units is the more accurate figure, because that is where most Indigenous women spend their time" (email message to author, September 2019). When this amount of $600,000 is multiplied by the number of incarcerated Indigenous women in Canada (9,460), the cost of incarcerated Indigenous women is then $5,676,000,000 per year ($5.676 billion).

In *Firewater: How Alcohol Is Killing My People (And Yours)*, Harold R. Johnson expresses how industries such as health care, police, judiciary and social services "depend upon our continued suffering" (2016), which leads me to question the motives and logic of the systems involved in the over-representation of Indigenous women in prison.

While addressing the vulnerability of Indigenous women through patterns of colonialism, my research also explores the judiciary's possible expectations with regards to recidivism from this cost analysis.

The literature reviewed indicates "how the complex processes of law are a disembodied discourse in which legal agents make the choices to utilize strategies to racialize and criminalize certain groups of people" (Maidment 2009). Groups included are: Indigenous women, single mothers, impoverished people (including women), the disabled and defenceless, and minorities. The author, MaDonna Maidment, identifies the construction of the "dangerous mother profile" and "think dirty" fabrications, and author Elizabeth Comack relates other labels, such as "unstable woman" and "loose woman," which continue to be used in the reasoning for stayed charges (2004). Comack, a professor in the Department of Sociology at the University of Manitoba, relates in *The Power to Criminalize* that law reforms are written in a rhetoric that depicts the equality which the judiciary states as their primary commitment, but the reality is the inequalities and injustices remain. (2004)

The major difference between staying and withdrawing charges is that when one's charges are stayed, they can be brought back to the court within one year; withdrawing is a permanent closure.

For the purpose of this research project, recidivism is defined as reconviction, because it requires a plea of finding of guilt in the court system and includes lesser crimes (such as stealing a loaf of bread) to the more serious crimes. The defining factors of the term recidivism are not clear in the research accessed to date. For one, an offender who is charged federally on one occasion, and provincially on a second crime at a later date, is not counted as re-offence. In some research, the discharged offenders are tracked for recidivism for periods ranging from one to three years. If a person is convicted for a crime following the expiry date of the tracking period, it is not necessarily deemed recidivism. The manner in which the offences are tabulated, federally and provincially, would actually drive the numbers of recidivism upwards, making the reported totals inaccurate.

There are other motivators that render this topic controversial. For one, disempowerment in its many forms makes a population impressionable, and in the same context, those who do not have the means of defending themselves become targets. Tuhiwai Smith uses the term "rounded up" to describe those being targeted for this purpose, falling victim to targeting and disempowerment through discriminatory and colonial practices.

~~~~~~

1.1 SITUATING MYSELF IN THIS RESEARCH

As a social worker within various populations in Ontario, I often work with clients who are seeking guidance and reassurance that the justice system will not criminalize them unnecessarily. I tell a story of a high-profile case in particular, the community will not be identified. However, for such a small community, and the augmented police presence on that particular day, it was obvious that many people would be charged. One new client was referred to me the following day because she had been wrongfully charged for selling drugs. The woman was advised to obtain a blood sample immediately, to rule out drug use. She felt that she was being charged for being in the presence of a drug dealer. I felt that fighting the charge would be drawn out for a long and expensive period of time, so instead I chose to refute the accusations by process of elimination. The blood test disproved the charge of drug use, which added credibility to her innocence. During that raid within the whole community, many people were charged. My client felt that her charge of dealing was wrongful because she was residing with her relative who was a drug dealer. The guilt by association was disproven but the unfortunate part of such a story is that the woman will never regain the five thousand dollars she had to pay for legal fees once her charges were dropped.

My Spirit name, Niibe Baape Kwe (Laughing Water Woman), and the teachings I have acquired, guide my journey here. Countless times I have reminded myself, *I can work around this*, as I envision flowing water contouring a blockage. Whether the blockage is deliberate, systemic, or egotistical, the water will find a way to flow. When the Elder Julie Ozawagosh suggested I "get to know my Spirit name" (personal communication, August 2009), I didn't like everything I found. In my life I have struggled to be "average," have wanted a common name, aspired to think as others do. My introspection taught me that water has many forms. Water can be liquid, solid, or vapour; cold, warm, or hot; soothing, calm, treacherous, and strong. Water gives life and takes life. Having acquired a deep appreciation for the qualities of water, I apply these in my work in order to understand situations, and to be a helper.

My literary projects and research are guided by the principles of water. Some of my statements will encompass the soothing nature of water, and my truth will be reflected, while other research findings that I relate are hard and unyielding.

1.2 RESEARCH OBJECTIVE

The objective is to critically explore the strategies that the judiciary and legislature, including politics, have at their disposal to influence a cycle of incarceration, criminalization, and recidivism as a means of forecasting the financial allocations required to satisfy the industries and various employment sectors directly and indirectly involved in the operational processes of the prison system.

1.3 RESEARCH DESIGN AND METHODOLOGY

The methodology in this project is informed by historical philosophies, as the chosen authors continue to be prominent today in academia. In order to advance a subject, it is felt that such historical ideologies must be critically examined and utilized as a framework for a possible trajectory or motive that is also consistent with the tenets of other theoretical perspectives used in this project. For example, to confidently express the contemporary methods of restorative justice practices, exploring the origins of such a method is necessary. This statement does not imply that restorative justice systems are necessarily new in Canada; some concepts date back historically. My primary research method involves the examination of entrenched literary history as a means of determining whether or not history is repeating itself regarding the disempowerment of women. The historical components I am referring to are the various methods of disempowerment that have been used, such as residential schools, the Sixties Scoop, women's forced relocations, etc. In essence, the disempowerment process is being repeated but under a different veil.

As a commitment in this written work, I abide by the highest standard of integrity observed in the Seven Grandfather Teachings: respect, truth, honesty, love, humility, courage, and wisdom.

The research for this work is text-based and qualitative.

Chapter 2

2.1 JUDICIAL AND POLITICAL PERSPECTIVES

The author Harold R. Johnson relates, in *Peace and Good Order* (2019), that Canada's judiciary relies on the principle of deterrence. However, the Solicitor General of Canada commissioned a study in 2002 looking at 111 studies involving 442,000 offenders, according to Johnson. The study concluded that people are more likely to reoffend the longer the original prison sentence was. Johnson also stresses that "the more we rely upon incarceration, the more we are forced to incarcerate" (2019, 98).

Who benefits from incarceration? Johnson explains that offenders do not heal from the historical traumas that led them to a life of crime. Johnson himself retells a story of a sexual assault committed upon him as a child. He explains that the process of reporting the crime now, and undergoing a trial, would re-traumatize him, thus setting him back on his healing journey. As a victim, Johnson feels that a judicial process would be a futile attempt at reconciliation; he adds that his assailants may get two years in prison, while the roots of the criminal behaviour may never be addressed (2019, 99).

In such an example, and in my perspective, the beneficiaries of incarceration are the numerous employment sectors—not the victim, nor the offenders, nor the community. The process Johnson describes is a method that abides by a ceaseless motion with no foreseeable healing outcome.

As a Crown prosecutor, Johnson tabulates the one thousand files he prosecutes per year multiplied by the eleven other prosecutors in the territory, all documenting multiple traumas at each court case. Within a few years, the citizens of that territory are at risk of being traumatized multiple times each, not just by their own court case, but by others within the community.

Accounting for the absence and deficiency of alternatives in many communities, Johnson cites the definition of insanity attributed to Albert Einstein, where one "[does] the same thing over and over again expecting a different result" (103).

From the perspective of a defence lawyer and prosecutor, Johnson expresses that law enforcement does not work and has not been working for "a thousand years," yet the same processes to initiate change in the story of law are repeated over and over. Johnson explains that—with the political elections and the audience's desires for harsher penalties—the amendments to the Criminal Code can then be counted as a victory within the political interests.

In game theory, agents (players) continually formulate alternative strategies in order to compete. To achieve this end, and within the definition of game theory, tools for decision-making processes are used accordingly to accommodate the fluctuations in a relevant content (Dixit and Nalebuff 2008). Scott Clark, in *Overrepresentation of Indigenous People in the Canadian Criminal Justice System: Causes and Responses*, relates that "despite the research and policy recommendations resulting from these inquiries, academia, and other sources, the problem of Indigenous over-representation continues and, in some ways, continues to worsen" (2019, 31). The inquiries Clark refers to are the eleven Royal Commissions of Inquiry since 1989. To add to the fluctuations amidst the definition of game, the Aboriginal Justice Inquiry of Manitoba (1991) states that, "It is not merely that the justice system has failed Aboriginal people; justice has also been denied to them" (Clark 2019, 6).

Johnson insists that the problem must be examined in context, taking into consideration "things to which the problem is connected" (2019, 129) if the rational solution is to be found. One of the points worth mentioning here, according to Johnson, is that the story of law has two adversarial sides within the system and they "decide which answer they want before they look at the problem" (2019, 88-89). The other point encompasses seven elements that are related to what Clark identifies as causes of over-representation: "colonialism; socio-economic marginalization; systemic discrimination; policing; courts; corrections; and culture clash" (Clark 2019, 13). These causes have extensive roots, and each could be a topic of research in itself. Johnson appears to exemplify that the "problem" could be named in simple terms. As an example only, let's call the problem addiction. In order to examine the problem of addiction, the seven elements that Clark lists must be further examined before a solution can be found. There are other ways that Johnson's statement could also be understood. If the problem, for example, is called violence, then the seven elements again could be examined further before a solution can be found. One of the methods that is gaining momentum in some courts is the Gladue Report, in which the historical elements that contribute to the present situation for individuals are being examined and considered. This may include colonialism, as well as socio-economic marginalization, which is only one effect of incarceration. Not all courts operate this way at the current time, but there is momentum being witnessed in many situations.

When I explore this concept within the context of political interest versus justice, I begin to recognize how each party may be driven from potential profitability. The political party aims to appease the communities' interest regarding job creation, sustainability, economic development, and business growth, to name a few. The judiciary has the knowledge and the methods to bring to fruition these political promises and aspirations. In 1989, the municipality of Oka was seeking to expand their golf course, despite the fact that the land in question infringed on the ancestral cemetery of the people of Kanehsatà:ke. Rather than encourage and participate in a resolution, the government's chosen tactics, including false allegations, were designed to alienate and direct support away from the Kanehsatà:ke community members. When a second injunction was granted to the municipality of Oka, police enforcement sought to remove the people from their ancestral community. The government and the judiciary had the methods and the means to bring an early resolution to this event, but they chose instead to fulfill the political promises that had been made and satisfy the town's desires to have a bigger golf course. (Katlatont Gabriel-Doxtater, Kawanatatie Van den Hende, 1995.) Ultimately, the land that had been occupied by Indigenous peoples for a few hundred years had been gaining value, and the expense of pushing the boundaries to gain that land was deemed worthwhile.

The judge, according to Johnson, is provided only the selected and deliberate pieces of evidence from the prosecutor, as well as the defence, which supports each argument. The judge's decision will be based on interpretations of the Charter of Rights and Freedoms and the Criminal Code of Canada, but these do not necessarily address the problem (Johnson, 2019, 88-89).

Within the judiciary, there is a term to describe a process of trickery that police and lawyers use to obtain a statement or a plea from the accused, regardless of its truth and validity. Even though the legal term is "plea bargaining," which is a process between the justice officials and the accused, the judiciary cannot be held accountable for the outcome. In particular, there is no assurance that the Crown fulfills the promises offered in the plea bargain (Department of Justice Bill C-15A). In such an instance, the accused may be offered a three-month sentence if they accept a plea bargain, versus five years if the matter is decided in a trial. Further, a guilty plea must be rendered by the accused before their case can be considered by the Gladue Courts. In essence, if the accused wants the Gladue report to be prepared and considered in court, and chooses a plea bargain in case a trial returns a very long sentence, they must plead guilty. The problem is that the guilty plea can never be reversed, even if the question was misunderstood, if the accused did not understand the consequences of their guilty plea, or if the accused is innocent.

Clark elaborates in his paper the various aspects that give rise to instances of miscommunication in the Item 4.4 Culture Clash (2019). Some of the elements described include the understanding of the concepts of justice versus Western concepts of justice; lack of knowledge from the courts to recognize Indigenous values; the diversities in worldview between Indigenous people and non-Indigenous people; the various methodologies that focus on rehabilitation as opposed to Western processes of punishment; incorrect assumptions of understanding which lead to inappropriate decisions (23).

From the work of Harold R. Johnson, I tend to believe his statistics and tabulations more than other research material. As a prior Crown prosecutor, who, in his words, has been "colonized sufficiently," Johnson relates two realities within the justice system in Canada. The first is the perspective of an Indigenous person; Johnson speaks of lived experiences: racism, judgments, and belittlement of his cultural worldview. The second is the fiction "that law is complex and only a select few are capable of succeeding in the profession" (22). From this broad understanding, Johnson expresses that "when a human is given power over other humans, there is a tendency to abuse that power" (2019). He expresses, with humility, that during his learning journey as a new lawyer, he worked tirelessly to prevent incarceration of Indigenous people. Johnson further explains certain cases he was defending where the accused should justifiably be incarcerated as a means of assuring safety and betterment for the family and the community. In a few years, and within this context, Johnson relates that "the more we rely upon incarceration, the more we are forced to incarcerate"(98). Options and resolutions are not being fully considered by the courts even when the methods of alternative justice do exist. Vicki Chartrand exemplifies this point but affirms that the accused could also voice their preference of retribution.

In my understanding of this statement, Johnson is expressing the predestined channels that the justice system has carved out, assuring predictable outcomes. Already the absence and deficiency of tributaries, in the form of alternative justice, becomes evident. When water flows from a carved-out channel (a river), the imminent tributaries (options) will receive the flow, but if no tributaries have been established, the flow will predictably arrive in the destined pool.

The justice system that Johnson describes follows a similar flow to arrive at the predictable destination. Within an understanding of deficiency of alternative channels, which could serve a population, such as recovery models and community initiatives, the system can and will reap the monetary benefits of a predictable system. I question what the motivation for the judiciary could be to insist upon a repeated method if the results clearly indicate and prove that the situation is getting worse. Johnson insists that "jail is not just the removal of a person from greater society, it is also the removal of their power of choice" (104) .

In *the Light of Justice: The Rise of Human Rights in Native America*, featuring the "UN Declaration on the Rights of Indigenous Peoples" (2007), Walter R. Echo-Hawk supports the phenomena of oppression, which includes a "diminished legal status for women" (2013, V) on a massive scale. The patterns of domination he relates are entrenched in the past and present socio-economic gaps, founded by practices of colonization (VIII). Echo-Hawk asserts that the continued systemic failures—creating the inequitable standards of living faced by Indigenous people— are created by an imaginary claim that obliging obedience is akin to legislation. Tuhiway Smith mirrors this sentiment in her term "rounded up." (2008)

By definition, coercion and assimilation are closely related and defined. Coercion involves the practice of persuasion to act and behave in a certain manner by using force or threats. By the same token, assimilation is a campaign to forcibly demand a certain behaviour from a group or person—usually a group.

The practice of assimilation of Indigenous people began during the 19th and 20th centuries, and continuing until 1996, when the last Canadian Indian residential school was closed in Canada. The consolidation of power over Indigenous land used methods and tactics such as the negotiation of treaties and the use of force. The outcome was the eventual isolation of Indigenous peoples to reserves. Upon the institution of a residential school system, the system made use of coercion to separate children from their families. Assimilation practices within these schools would work to abolish their traditional language and expression of culture.

This type of administration was subsequently intertwined with the Sixties Scoop, wherein children were forcibly removed from their families and their communities to be sent to foreign (Canadian or otherwise) homes and families. I am using this example to emphasize how, under a veil of human rights, the actions and intentions were to coerce and assimilate. The phases of removal and family estrangement continued when women were removed from their communities under the guise of matrimonial focus. Indigenous women who had married non-Indigenous men were forced to leave their reserves and be stripped of their ancestral kinship. By definition, this practice was a campaign of coercion and assimilation, as these women were forced to adopt non-Indigenous status.

The recurring or rhythmic pattern of coming and going can now be witnessed within the system of incarceration, where women are coerced into a life of disempowerment, assimilation, and belittlement—to name only a few of the descriptions I have heard spoken by women who've experienced it. The pattern of decline and regrowth can also be witnessed in the rate of recidivism for Indigenous women within the prison system, as mentioned earlier.

According to Echo-Hawk, "The UN goal to uplift socio-economic conditions of Indigenous people is compatible with the 'American Dream'" (2013), although the ideals within this concept include economic security, employment, health, and housing, and such prosperity for Indigenous people is illusive.

The phenomenon of "otherness" is explained as a construction of difference embedded in policy and law. The aim is to "debase" culture in order to impose transformation in the "other." When I attempt to define the word "debase," I envision a structure being disembarked from its original foundation, which had a purpose of assuring strength, stability, and form. In the social context, the definition of "debase" holds the intent of reducing the value and soundness of an entity: a person, group, culture, and worldview. In essence, in the absence of a foundation—which culture and belief systems had assured for people—the construct of a daily life, encompassing quality and predictability, becomes impossible to achieve. Echo-Hawk exemplifies this.

Harold R. Johnson relates the words spoken at an Elders gathering where a woman "asserts that in her experience the problems in her community could be traced to two causes: the imposition of welfare and the justice system" (2016, 144). These two forces had imposed "uncaring bureaucracies . . . to serve their own purpose (2016, 144). Echo-Hawk relates that there are barriers preventing the attainment of UN standards in the USA (Echo-Hawk 2013), which include the legal disregard in the development of traditional economies, and the complacency and inaction of government. As Johnson stated, "Why would they if the machine is well oiled and running" (2019).

Echo-Hawk further explains that statement through the lens of colonialism and conquest:

1. Government can curtail self-determination at will; and

2. Non-discrimination in the law appears unattainable as long as the principles of colonialism form part of the judiciary (2013).

Clark parallels Echo-Hawk's thoughts when he cites the work of Michael Jackson for the Canadian Bar Association. In a report, he spoke:

> . . . of a colonial relationship whereby cultural alienation, territorial dispossession, and socio-economic marginalization became increasingly pronounced among Indigenous peoples. According to Jackson, "[t]his process of dispossession and marginalization has carried with it enormous costs of which crime and alcoholism are but two items on a long list" (1988: 218). In other words, the impacts of colonialism have contributed in significant ways to the over-representation of Indigenous people in the criminal justice system (2019, 14).

In *When Justice Is a Game: Unravelling Wrongful Convictions in Canada*, Maidment exemplifies the ways in which the state rationalizes a prosecution, even a wrongful one, under the shadow of the Charter of Rights and Freedoms (2009). Maidment relates how the state has access to "limitless financial and other resources and not necessarily the costs preceding the imprisonment." This example serves to highlight the fallible nature and the possible distortions of the workings of the justice system.

Wrongful convictions occur up to ten times as often in marginalized populations, according to Maidment. She explains that middle-class targets are more expensive to coerce. However, they do occur, as police, prosecutors, and judges collaborate in the tragic construction of a prosecution (2009).

In the history of Criminal Law, the Blackstone ratio (also known as Blackstone formulation) from 1760 is the idea that "it is better that ten guilty persons escape than that one innocent suffer." The idea was subsequently incorporated into the legal jurisdictions, including law school, even though the statement continues to be a topic of debate. The statement insists that government and the judiciary must err on the side of innocence (Epp 2015). Common law continues to be influenced by this phrase, however, in the case of over-representation of Indigenous women in prison, the opposite is suggested.

The term "justice is blind" appears in various texts reviewed for this book. Maidment emphasizes this term when she tabulates the cost of the public inquiries initiated from wrongful convictions in Canada over time. Add to this the compensation awarded to eight men at the centre of the inquiries for an astronomical cost exceeding $70 million (2009). However, she points out that the various costs to gain a conviction, the numerous appeals, and the costs of incarceration are not included in this tally.

The social, legal, and political dimensions of wrongful convictions are interpreted and framed in the same manner as the
marginalized population are incarcerated in the current time. By
this statement I am explaining that the resolve and drive applied
to achieve conviction hold the same intensity as the desire to
incarcerate people: the ferocity to win at all costs. These, along
with the systemic biases which converge to tragically construct a
"profile" of Indigenous women, form part of the judiciary's conviction—thus, the miscarriage of justice. It appears to be a game
for certain experts, as can be witnessed in the examples of marginalized women. In 1994, pathologist Dr. Smith told the Canadian
Press that "his forensic unit had a higher batting average . . . when
it came to getting convictions against child killers" (Anderson
and Anderson 2009), higher average meaning a conviction rate
compared to other professionals who aim for the same outcome.
From the cited statement, I am understanding that Dr. Smith
interpreted his success in obtaining convictions to a game of base-
ball (he is deeming himself the best player). In this news report,
Charles Randal Smith was discovered performing flawed child
autopsies that resulted in wrongful convictions. While working
at the Hospital for Sick Children in Toronto, he had performed
more than one thousand child autopsies from 1982 to 2003. Of
these autopsies, between thirteen and twenty resulted in criminal
charges for the guardian or parent. This prompted the Goudge
Inquiry, in which it was discovered that Smith had reported misleading information and statements in court, leading to further
wrongful convictions.

Smith proclaimed that he had "a thing against people who hurt
children," while critics said that "he was on a crusade and acted
more like a prosecutor" than a pathologist (1). This serves as an
example of how the system—conceptualized to appease poverty
and all its associated ills—has turned out to be a lucrative playing
field for many.

As a means to convict, and in spite of the financial pool available, the judiciary relies on certain contributors, including "the misuse of jailhouse informants; nondisclosure by the Crown and police; false and forced confessions; eye witness misidentification; misuse of expert evidence; unreliable scientific evidence; mishandling of alibi witnesses; institutional elements of police culture, forensic facilities, trial and appellate courts; inadequate legal aid funding; inadequate defence work; and misleading circumstantial evidence" (Maidment 2009). According to Maidment, predisposing factors can be added, such as "systemic racism, class biases toward the poor, sensationalism of crimes and political collaboration in the form of crime control strategies." As a social response, women have been criminalized and labelled as "deviant" in the absence of society's definition of maternal construct. Maidment relates that within the "parenting norms," defiance has also been termed "motherhood offence." Maidment is explaining that any act of defiance committed by a mother, and which falls outside society's definition of parenting norms, will be defined as motherhood offence.

Here is a personal example: when my children were in secondary school, all children were disallowed to wear their winter boots as opposed to their inside shoes when relocating from the main school building to the annex classrooms on the property. I had a discussion with the principal to inform her that my children would be wearing their boots if they were cold. The principal stated that the rule was made by the school board and it could not be changed. I informed her, "My kids will wear their boots," The principal rose from her chair and stood at her office door indicating that I leave the meeting. In the school's perception, I was being defiant. There were no consequences from the school that I was made aware of, but my children communicated that I stop raising those issues. In many instances in everyday life, mothers are disallowed to voice their concerns. Those that do are labelled defiant. In Northern communities, when transportation is expensive for people to attend court in another city, their absence is deemed defiant.

This form of social control has far-reaching effects, including poverty, criminalization, inequality, inadequate childcare, and inadequate housing, all of which are directly and indirectly related to the determinants of health.

If the game strategy is dominant, all others are dominated; this concept appears in methods of colonialism and control. There are components within game theory, including symmetric/ asymmetric strategy, simultaneous/sequential and cooperative/ uncooperative types. As an example, the uncooperative type can be exemplified in the way rational economic agents deal with each other to achieve their own goals. In the 1960s and 1970s, when Indigenous women who had married non-Indigenous men were removed from their communities, the economic benefits for the agents translated into lesser monetary obligations, reduced paperwork in the form of status cards; as well, the systems succeeded in their goal of diminishment of the Indigenous population by allowing non-Indigenous women to reside in that community. The simultaneous/sequential strategy can also be personified from that example in that within the same effort and command for Indigenous women to leave, the action of non-Indigenous women were allowed to remain. A sequential method could have occurred if the agents making that rule had considered the implications that would be forthcoming, even decades later. Asymmetrical strategies are characterized by the strike on the vulnerabilities of a population or group, those that have limited opportunity to defend themselves.

In a symmetrical strategy, a zero sum aim always produces an equilibrium for the parties involved, which means that communication and consideration are afforded to all. This reminds me of politics. In these types, I recognize the workings of colonialism from past to present, the way agents use strategies to influence and predict a marginalized population's behaviour so that the best action for their gain can be deliberately chosen.

Game theory is widely used in the disciplines of economics and business, psychology, and many others. Therefore, the advent of pangs of hunger become the pawn of manipulation consistent with the strategies of the game. I draw a parallel between Arendt's concept of non-humanitarian strategies and some components of game theory when exemplifying the advent of pangs of hunger. The literature accessed in this research exemplifies countless examples of Indigenous populations who were offered land, farming equipment, and living necessities in exchange for the relinquishment of their Indigenous status. The groups of people retold in the book *At the Wood's Edge* are a good example. They were offered relocation to Ontario and promised housing, building supplies, food, living necessities, and employment. What they encountered in reality was the absence of all those promised goods. The agents who reneged on their promises appear to have strategically considered that the people would have no means to return to their community, nor the means to live with some comfort such as shelter and food, therefore the pangs of hunger became a pawn to coerce obedience and compliance. Countless industries benefit and profit from the predictions explained earlier, in terms of recidivism. Therefore, hunger and substandard quality of life are subjective. Arendt explains the "urgency of needs to whose existence or non-existence nobody can ever testify except the one who happens to suffer them" (1998, 120). Arendt explains by that statement that hunger is a "reality in the life process itself" (1998, 120). Using the earlier example of relocated people to Nipissing area, the public admiration would be assigned to the agents who orchestrated the reduced population by relocating them. Arendt asserts that the hunger can be defined by the lived experience of the people, and not by the agents who were being admired for their political achievements.

In 1869 there were "penalties of opinion" (Mill 2006, xxviii) that still exist in the current time. Mill was aware that public opinion that influenced government would "enact public prejudice into law" (xxvii). He explains, however, that "the agent's own good is not a valid reason for compelling him to act one way rather than another, nor is our belief that he would be a better person" (xxviii). The penalties of opinion that Mill asserts can be likened to the current society's voice to increase safety and punishment in terms of the deemed motherhood offences (and other examples of defiance). Even though the perceived political achievements towards these ends may elevate the agents' esteemed good, it still only remains as a penalty of opinion. Mill asserts that, in 1869, the action of coercing obedience had to be justified, with proof indicating harm to others or all. The current rate of incarceration for Indigenous women exemplifies that point. He emphasizes "that the principle applies only to coercion, and it applies to all forms of it" (xxviii).

Wesley Cragg and Christine M. Koggel (2005) assert core values when discussing contemporary moral issues. The three following principles, introduced in the first chapter of Contemporary Moral Issues, are the protection-of-life principle, the avoidance of suffering principle, and the moral-autonomy principle. Cragg and Koggel explain that although suffering is a feature humans strive to deter, "there is a moral obligation to help others alleviate suffering when possible." By the same token, freedom to act is meant to be "compatible with others having an equal degree of freedom to do the same." The fourth principle introduced in the chapter on equality and discrimination is "the principle of equal worth." The authors express that this principle is pertinent to the remainder of the book. Groups and individuals witness the imposition of discrimination and the effects of unequal treatment in many facets of life. The examples are entrenched in historical accounts, even though the charters, bills, and declarations of human rights are conscientiously written to reverse the effects of such intrusive practices. Cragg and Koggel raise profound questions when exploring issues of conflict regarding the principles of equal worth. One such query explores the extent of various manifestations, which "determine in advance the life prospects and goals" of individuals and groups.

To further Cragg and Koggel's thought, the process that I term "deliberate infringement" explains how the strategies of game theory repeatedly and purposefully curtail the autonomy and self-worth of Indigenous women. This process of restriction can be seen in the high rates of recidivism and incarceration.

In the book *Good Reasons for Better Arguments: An Introduction to the Skills and Values of Critical Thinking* (Bickenbach and Davies 1997), it is asserted that formal logic "promises certainty about its conclusions." The authors argue that the word "critical" derives from the Greek word "krino," defined as "to decide or judge something," emphasizing that the "decisive" moment does not hold as much value as the "process that leads to the judgments and decisions." In essence, the process of evaluating the way the judgment was formulated holds relevance when defining "critical thinking."

We must consider the reasoning of the judiciary and the state when it comes to their decisions to criminalize Indigenous women. Although it does create some discomfort to argue which practice is critically sound in a democratic society, it would be erroneous not to question the integrity of my opinion versus the judiciary's when the lives of people are at stake.

Bickenbach and Davies further explain what economists call "cost-benefit analysis" (1997). This analysis is a "tool for securing the aim or goal of economic efficiency—using resources in a way that achieves the greatest benefits at the lowest cost." However, the authors express that cost-benefit analysis does not indicate "why efficiency should be a social value, or how it ranks among other important social values" (1997).

2.2 A THEORETICAL PERSPECTIVE

The theoretical perspective asserted in this chapter is essentially a synthesis of ideas drawn from numerous theories, whether in social work, philosophy, or otherwise, presented together to be understood as a comparison. The symmetrical analogy in this statement exemplifies how one concept defined in a particular faculty is synonymous with the enhanced definitions from another, yet they remain similar in meaning and intent. For example, the tenets of systems theory—meaning the cohesiveness of services and resources who collaborate towards an outcome in a context of social work can be mirrored as systems in philosophy whose interests lie in the realities aiming to resolve human issues in a greater context.

In order to improve any practice, we are assigned the task of advancing assumptions into theories, making use of an analysis of common factors that can be measured in terms of viability. This can be said of theories from any and all disciplines.

In *The Human Condition,* Hannah Arendt uses "the historian" as a character who is well positioned to assess or interpret all the facets of a particular situation. Arendt relates that "even though stories are the inevitable results of action, it is not the actor but the storyteller, in this case the historian, who perceives and 'makes' the story." This analogy is provided here to demonstrate how policies and procedures have been formulated historically but have neglected to critically analyze the various facets of the "story in the making." The "story in the making" in this book involves the many efforts and initiatives that have adversely affected Indigenous women for the past two hundred years.

In the story of residential schools, for example, I question whether theories of human advancement—such as person-centred approaches or empowerment approaches—were considered in its formulation. Some of the foundational principles of person-centred approaches revolve around "the importance of individuality, trust in feeling and intuition, and nonauthoritarian relationships" (Rowe and Turner 1996). Carl Rogers, one of the early and prominent coordinators of the principles of person-centred theory, was instrumental in advancing "humanism," as it was "related to his belief that humans are essentially growth-oriented, forward-moving, and concerned with fulfilling their basic potentialities" (Rowe and Turner 1996).

By the same token of advancement, in *The Empowerment Approach to Social Work Practice*, Lee cites Germain and Gitterman (1979, 1991) in explaining that the empowerment approach "adopts the ecological perspective . . . which helps us to see the interdependence of all living and nonliving systems and the transactional nature of relationships" (Lee, Turner, 1996). The approach is built on the foundation that there is a "goodness of fit between people and environments" (Lee, Turner, 1996). Lee also elaborates that "by definition, poor people and oppressed groups seldom have this 'fit,' as injustice stifles human potential" (Lee, Turner, 1996).

As stated in subsequent chapters, the 'fit' that Gitterman exemplifies in the person-environment exchanges does hold the opportunity to provide lasting improvement if the conditions are ideal. The stifling that Lee discusses is a direct result of the dysfunctional responses, geared to an eventual disintegration. In essence, incarceration can be the parasitic environment; dysfunction grows in the absence of a healthy person-environment fit.

Mary Valentich quotes Collins in Feminist Theory and Social Work Practice: "Social work's emphasis on the person-in-environment is congruent with the central methodological theme of feminism—the personal is the political" (Valentich 1996). Yet another theory promotes and is grounded in the person-environment philosophy. In essence, an individual and their behaviour must be understood through the lens of their environment, the physiological aspects as well as the relational facets of the environment, including the larger systems—law, healthcare, history, and politics—and how discrimination impacts a woman's needs and how she views the world. One aspect of the ecological theory blends well with the feminist theory, in that the interactions between the individual and their environment is indicative of the woman's overall functioning, gathered by her interpretation of her environment and the experiences within it. The feminist theory draws heavily on the reality that is formulated from the influences in the environment. For a person who is incarcerated, the home, work, and school facets all occur within that institution. On a deeper level, a person's reaction to the responses from people in her environment all influence one another, and it depends on whether the interactions within the environment are positive or negative (working together or working against each other).

There are numerous other perspectives and theories that have the power to affect the well-being of women who are incarcerated and that contradict the conditions of her environment, such as historical events in a person's life, the ability to identify ways to achieve her goals and strengths, even if they must be found within their struggles. The contradiction is that the actions initiated with the purported intention to protect society are actually destroying the well-being of a population (nationwide or otherwise). In the workings of social work theory, the strengths found amidst a struggle has potential to occur with the use of Strength-Based or Client-Centered approaches. Without denying the historical realities that have occurred in Canada, many Indigenous people rise above the atrocities using different methods (higher education, creativity, etc.). The contradiction that I am referring to has been witnessed historically (and continues today) in the exclusion of women from politics, management, decision-making processes, freedom, and inherent abilities that have always been upheld within Indigenous communities. This contradiction originates from the authoritarian structure aiming for disempowerment of women. The person-environment fit is then erased. A contradiction that becomes evident, not as a social work mishap, but more so from an authoritarian structure, is precisely the origin of the neglect-in-design within the relentless process of incarceration. Current reform and retribution systems have not critically considered the facets of the person-environment fit, the consequences of stifling a person's advancement within that same fit, growth-oriented objectives, or the conditions necessary for achievement of personal potential.

Game theory, as a supposition of ideas, is widely used in the disciplines of economics and business and many other disciplines. As a strategic proposition making use of the principles of interest, rights, and power, it is also a structure invested in predicting behaviours (Dixit and Nalebuff 2008). Game theory does contain its perils, in that with the introduction of decisive points in any game, the rules tend to be renegotiated or changed, which is witnessed in many contemporary issues involving interactions between Indigenous communities and the State.

The primary tenets of game theory are the players, determinability, the information action available to each, strategy, decision points, the payoffs for each outcome, player skill, rationality, and maximization. In economics, for example, game theory helps to describe, predict, and explain people's behaviours (Dixit and Nalebuff 2008).

There are some limitations to game theory: The strategies available to each player are not always known. Guess work is a relevant tactic for each player.

The tenets stated above can be summarized in one example: Treaty rights. There are countless statements, meanings, promises, and intents which continue, to this day, to be misconstrued. The players are always the same, Agents vs. Indigenous populations. The strategies are by far not always well-defined (if at all), and neither are the decision points. The longstanding issues that many Indigenous communities continue to experience regarding their drinking water system is a good example.

The non-consensual sterilization that Indigenous women have been subjected to since the 1970s is another concrete example that falls within the imposed limitations of rationality and decision points within game theory. The intended sterilization by the medical professionals was not communicated to the women. They had been scheduled for other minor surgery and in which time, the sterilization was performed without consent. The tenets of Game Theory in this context depicts the absence of communication between the parties; that the rules be interchangeable without notice; that the decision points (scheduled surgery) make use of the strategies which will affect the outcome (by the medical group); and the rewards which can be defined (subordination, coercion, obedience).

When I apply the principles of game theory to the topic of overrepresentation of Indigenous women in prison, I explore how the players—such as the judiciary, the state, and the specific marginalized population—are not necessarily on a common playing field (Dixit and Nalebuff 2008). However, that may be part of the strategy of contemporary colonization.

Critical theory also informs this written work, in that it encompasses a pragmatic goal to identify and transcend the circumstances that limit human freedom. The objectives of critical theory can be appreciated only through interdisciplinary research that includes social dimensions and inquiry, cultural understandings, and psychological and institutional forms of domination (Nash and Munford 2009). A paradox is created when the many facets of social control are applied in conjunction with critical theory, considering that the penal technique is a method of social control through law—a direct contradiction to freedom.

In *Social Work Practice: Problem Solving and Beyond*, "power in feminism is seen as a flexible resource that enables people's empowerment, and it can be extended and shared" (Heinonen and Spearman 2010). Power over people, as in domination, is far removed from this definition. Feminism focuses on "power within a person" (2010), which aims to form an alliance with other schools of thought to enhance a purposeful outcome for all.

Critical thinking takes a philosophical approach: "Logic is sometimes called the science of the laws of thought" (Bickenbach and Davies 1997). In support of this process, some authors express that "to make an argument is to give reasons in support of a conclusion" (Bickenbach and Davies 1997), explaining that in order to enhance the formulation of a conclusion, "The key . . . is to view it as a form of communication." This approach adds weight to the argument that communication is not always a priority when certain rules of game theory are applied.

Chapter 3

3.1 POVERTY AS A PRODUCT OF INCARCERATION

The word "consequence" can be broadly defined as a result of both a condition and an action. Within the profession of social work and the discipline of psychology, consequence is the response that follows an action which aims to modify a certain behaviour. To elaborate, consequence within the context of risk assessment is the impact created in the likelihood of an event occurring. The event in this research is defined as the deemed criminal activity or behaviour. Likelihood can be measured by how probable it is that a person will behave in a certain manner. This method of measurement is relevant if the enforcement of an action is present.

Justice Alvin C. Hamilton and C. Murray Sinclair indicate in the Public Inquiry into the Administration of Justice and Aboriginal People of Manitoba—also called the Aboriginal Justice Inquiry—"that the over-representation of Indigenous women in prison can be traced, in part, to victimization" (1991), even as children. They explain that in the interviews with Indigenous women, "Many felt trapped in an impossible economic and social situation from which there was little chance to escape" (Sinclair and Hamilton 1991).

Tuhiwai Smith argues that the "indigenous problem" became "embedded as a policy discourse" once the peoples had been "rounded up" and became subjects of social control. From this perspective, the Indigenous people were to blame for self-directed poverty, justified by a theory that Indigenous people had resisted the "terms of their colonization" (Tuhiwai Smith 2008). Tuhiwai Smith expresses that "within the regimes of colonialism, survival is the pressing issue." She relates that amidst the generational cycles of poverty, people are "fed messages about their worthlessness, laziness, dependence, and lack of 'higher' order of human qualities." Tuhiwai Smith affirms that this method of oppression is paralleled within Indigenous communities in nations in all stages of development. However, within the constructs of social control, it appears, in my view, that the impositions of oppression, forced relocations, deprivation of services, and many more, are nothing short of neglectful.

Much has been written in regards to the gendered lens the judiciary uses in sentencing. In *Implicating the System*, Elspeth Kaiser-Derrick relates that in the judicial discourses in the sentencing of indigenous women, "The Royal Commission on Aboriginal Peoples (RCAP) concluded in 1996 that 'the over-representation is linked directly to the particular and distinctive historical and political processes that have made Aboriginal people poor beyond poverty, in a deeply entrenched process of colonization'" (Kaiser 2019, 2). Kaiser-Derrick borrows the term "feminization of poverty" from Gillian Balfour (*Do Law Reforms Matter?*) to emphasize the neglectful manner in which cases are presented and interpreted in court, and how women are sentenced (Kaiser 2019). She relates that the multiple layers and diverse forms of victimization for Indigenous women include the "prevalence of state oppression" (Kaiser 2019), which parallels the statement from

Sherene H. Razack, indicating that we must "[put] the context back into law" (Kaiser 2019) in order for social change to occur.

In *Deviance, Conformity, and Social Control in Canada*, Tami M. Bereska relates how Emile Durkheim suggested in the Anomie Theory how the notion of deviance is functional "in helping maintain society's balance or equilibrium" (Bereska 2018). Bereska elaborates that "societal tensions can be reduced when there is some sort of scapegoat that can be blamed for a social problem, since blaming the scapegoat takes the pressure off society at large" (2018).

This example serves to depict one scenario of the cycle of poverty. The legal processes do not bear weight on this research. However, it serves to demonstrate one probable root of poverty. Once the woman is released from prison, the processes of re-establishing her life are also costly. Before she can have her children returned, the mother must secure housing; however, before she can secure housing, she must demonstrate financial soundness. In order to prove financial stability, she must have a revenue, which is sometimes impeded by her criminal record and the implications thereof; for example, her criminal record limits the choices in employment. The cycle is often repeated when the mother steals a loaf of bread (or performs another illegal activity) because she is compelled to care for her children. The co-commissioners Hamilton and Sinclair state, following interviews with incarcerated women, that "none of the women we spoke to wanted to be involved in criminal activity, but they often believed it was necessary to do so" (Hamilton and Sinclair 1991).

As a continued effort to bring light the notion of poverty leading to criminalization for Indigenous women, future case studies should be undertaken to examine the financial deprivation women endure when they are targeted for incarceration. The costs may include legal expenses, loss of housing, implications with child welfare agencies, childcare, loss of employment, future employability with a criminal record, and so much more. Each province and each system within the provinces has a spectrum of financial platforms, such as the grid people fall within in order to qualify for monthly revenue. The prolonged delays, the narrow qualifiers within the grid system, the notorious six- to eight-week waiting period to receive a copy of something from government, are all obstacles within a system aiming to provide for families. Yet, in the absence of revenue, and in the absence of personal identification (which is often lost in the midst of incarceration) and income tax assessment forms, the task of obtaining housing is greatly delayed.

In Canada, a progressive and democratic country, what are the roots that poverty grows from? The determinants of health in Canada—that of income and social status, employment, education and literacy, physical environments, childhood experiences, social supports and coping skills, healthy behaviours, and access to health services—are greatly reduced in the absence of adequate revenue (Health Canada 2020).

Elspeth Kaiser-Derrick draws from Joyce Green's definition of colonialism as "both an historic and a continuing wrong. A term that encompasses economic and political practices, it refers to the appropriation of the sovereignty and resources of a nation or nations, to the economic and political benefits of the colonizer. The practice by which colonialism is normalized and legitimated includes racism, which is encoded in law, policy, education, and the political and popular culture of the colonizer" (Kaiser-Derrick 2019). Kaiser-Derrick also draws on Gillian Balfour's statement about the "feminization of poverty," as both sides of the judiciary fail to "recognize the gendered conditions of endangerment in Aboriginal women's communities as a systemic factor" (Kaiser-Derrick 2019).

There are geniuses within many employment sectors who have sent people to the moon and beyond; surely there are geniuses who can tabulate methods to correct the social ills which continue to impose harm onto people. Poverty is only one of the many consequences of over-incarceration. A sense of self-worth, confidence, empowerment, desire, and ability to advance are some of the possible benefits that could ensue should a person be treated in a just manner. The cycles of incarceration, wrongful convictions, and recidivism could be avoided or reduced greatly with the application of some ingenuity.

This is exemplified in the statement from Laurie Monsebraaten (2018, 2020) quoting the Canada Injured Workers' Association (CIWA): "poverty results from systemic polarity rather than luck and poor choices." According to CIWA's research findings, the consequence of poverty is encountered from a condition which is firstly intentioned by the construct of an action, such as claim denial. CIWA's findings derive from the 2015 income tax data and the 2016 census from Statistics Canada (Monsebraaten 2018, 2020).

I would like to explain here that, from my understanding, a very small percentage of WSIB claims are accepted as valid. It is not a fact that is published anywhere. But I can see the agency's reasoning, that if all claims are accepted, the agency would be spending a lot of money on claims, and more people would be opening a claim. Having said that, the waiting period for a WSIB claim to be considered is approximately ten months or more. I know some people who have been waiting three years. For an injured worker, defined by the CIWA as one who is neither able to work nor be productive in life (i.e., obtain groceries), ten months is long enough to become very poor. Therefore, poverty is not a result of poor choices (in many cases) but rather a systemic construct to make people wait. Once people are fed up waiting, WSIB anticipate that people will accept some form of employment regardless of pain and/or limited mobility.

Notwithstanding the processes and the circumstances involved in sending a woman to prison, the financial implications are excessive. There are some common reasons to point the finger at causal factors of poverty, but in 2017, 9.5% of Canada's population lived in poverty. In context, that amounts to 3.47 million people (Statistics Canada 2018). There are numerous reasons for poverty: greed, theft, lack of education, natural disasters, injustice, oppression. These are only a few that come to mind. According to Statistics Canada, the bottom 90% of Canadians average an income of $28,000 gross per year; in context, this same population's net income is less than twenty thousand (Statistics Canada 2018).

In 2005, as a result of family court issues, as well as becoming a single mother of two teenagers, my revenue for the year was $6,200. From this revenue, I had to pay for rent, heating, food, and all the necessities for a family of three. On three occasions during that year, I applied for social assistance, because I did not have any money for any kind of transportation to obtain a job, as much as I wanted to work, while living on the outskirts of Sudbury, where rent was less costly. According to a social advocate—towards the end of a ten-month period—I had been denied social assistance because my prior "business name" remained active. This reasoning is not based on any form of business activity: just the name. It should be noted as well that following those three declined applications, I was not informed of those decisions. I don't know why such neglect is still practised, but there is no need for such behaviour from so-called professional agencies who are mandated to help people.

Poverty is comprised of many ill effects: immobilization, hunger, feelings of hopelessness, disempowerment, and interdependency, to name a few. Poverty should not be a goal or an aim.

3.2 THE EFFECTS ON CHILDREN

The cycles of behaviours that arise from the absence of a healthy attachment to a primary caregiver during childhood have been the subject of many studies within a wide spectrum of clinical disciplines. In *Social Work Theories in Action*, Nash, Munford, and O'Donoghue have included a chapter by Sue Watson about attachment theory (2009). The cycle described herein can be understood from a child's perspective, or a mother's. The causes described in this cycle are born from the repeated incarceration of Indigenous women or women in general. The effects of attachment are the same for all populations, but the rate of incarceration for Indigenous women is higher.

Attachment theory was born from the idea that both cognitive and emotional development of children depends on their experiences in early years. The parents' behaviour can have the long-term effects on the child, and that translates to the child's interpretation of a particular social environment. Defiance is one such effect. From a clinical paradigm, the brain develops through the interactions with its environment, thus the person-environment dynamic is born. Clinical research also indicates that deprivation or separation from a mother or primary caregiver has an effect on the child's future criminal disposition (Watson, 2009, 208). For the purpose of this book, no bias is imposed on either the mother or the child. When a mother is subjected to incarceration due to extreme poverty or other social ill, both the mother and the child experience the effects of incarceration.

Regarding the breath of life theory, Blackstock and Cross posit "self and community actualization, role, service, identity, and esteem" as the primary tenets of well-being and potential of growth, as is exemplified in the relational worldview model (Cross 1997; Cross, 2007). Blackstock expresses that "if the relational worldview principles are out of balance within the framework of community culture and context, then risks to the child's safety and well-being will increase." Blackstock and Cross's relational worldview principles (1997; 2007) demonstrate that an individual within the context of the community (not depicted in Maslow's theory), considers a "multi-generational community actualization versus an individual actualization and transcendence" (Blackstock 2007). This relevant finding emphasizes that all factors within the growth of an individual are "highly interdependent in nature with cultural values and laws defining how balance is achieved on personal and collective levels" (Blackstock 2007).

The relational model is "illustrated with a four-quadrant circle" representing "four major forces . . . that together must come into balance" (Blackstock 2007). The four major forces are also referred to as "sets of factors" (Blackstock 2007) and encompass "context, mind, body, and spirit" which are elaborated to distinguish how each factor contributes to the harmony "between the many interrelating factors in one's circle of life," thus called relational.

Bereska critiques the functionalist logic (2018) that institutions (apart from the institution of the family) are created to meet the needs to socialize children. Bereska reiterates that in the functionalist perspective, both the family and the education system may not be a practical approach in terms of simultaneous efforts to socialize and educate children. By keeping women in prison, the other institutions, such as the school system, fulfill their mandated functions, and the process of socializing Indigenous children is augmented.

To summarize, the research indicates that children have the ability to adapt and accept the circumstances in their life—however, family and community contribute extensively to their mental, emotional, and spiritual growth. When mothers are removed from the life of a child, the rate and the quality of development is noticeably reduced.

3.3 ISOLATION AND SEPARATION

Hannah Arendt exemplifies in *The Human Condition* that "action . . . is never possible in isolation; to be isolated is to be deprived of the capacity to act" (1998). In the chapter "The Frailty of Human

Affairs," Arendt discusses the similarities and differences between the origins of the words "to lead" and "to set in motion," and how isolation is a delusion; gains in the condition of the world cannot be achieved singularly and apart from human interactions. This delusion is based on the notion that women who are separated from others, including their children, have the capacity to be coerced into obedience and assimilation.

The perils of this notion of isolation are exemplified in most social work theories. Force will not produce exemplary results for the human race. What will likely result from isolation is a generation of adults who operate with a fear-based lens, thus there will be political and legal implications, where survival is at stake. The tenets of assimilation and colonialism ascribe to the notion that separation produces a desired outcome; this could possibly be named coercion.

However, the removal of women by any means, including the most intrusive and dehumanizing act of incarceration, which is disguised under a veil of limitations, can only result in "consequences which range from heroic adaptation, to impair functioning, to parasitic exploitation, to individual and collective disintegration" (Gitterman and Turner 1996). The collective, in this case, can be translated to the community, or the family, or the environment, or any other social circle. In essence, the disintegration that was anticipated and aimed for in the residential school scheme, and all other attempts of separation, shared the same principles of breakdown—and women were affected in all of them.

Gitterman discusses that the person-environment exchanges that are out of balance have the capacity to expand into a more frustrating, damaging situation unless the fit between the two can be improved (Gitterman 1996). The same is true of inmates within a person-environment context. If the person does not receive the essentials to their well-being—empathy, support, and understanding—the imbalance becomes evident. Gitterman further explains that when "coping efforts fail, physiological and emotional strains are intensified, which can lead to . . . immobilization, or dysfunctional . . . social responses. Dysfunctional responses generate more stressors . . . toward deterioration and disintegration." In essence, disintegration can be further defined as isolation and separation from the environment that was meant to offer support and empathy.

In a supportive environment, unlike the isolation of incarceration, the effective exchanges between people are more likely to influence all parties' responsiveness towards a good fit. Gitterman defines this latter thought as the "greatest opportunity for lasting improvement" (Gitterman, Turner 1996).

Chapter 4

4.1 COST ANALYSIS

When discussing cost benefits in any venture, many factors influence the evaluation aiming for an outcome or decision. When considering the elements of a cost analysis, the financial metrics, such as potential revenue and the possible cost savings as a result of a new project, can also include intangible benefits such as employee morale, inventory reduction, and customer satisfaction. To add to this intangible list, we can include favourable political relationships, a predictable revenue source as a benefit of relationships. An additional benefit to supplying large volumes of goods to a substandard client base involves the liquidation of discontinued and redundant inventory. If the forecasted benefits outweigh the costs, it could be a decisive opportunity to move forward with the project. On the other hand, if the costs surmount the benefits, the company may want to reconsider the project or venture.

In the topic of the $20 billion cost (as reported by John Howard Society, 2018) of incarcerating people in Canada, the breakdown per category includes salaries and employee benefits

(70%); utilities, materials, and supplies (9%); amortization of tangible capital assets (8%); professional and special services (6%); payment in lieu of taxes (2%); machinery and equipment (2%); repairs and maintenance (2%); all other expenses (1%). Of the $1.574 billion in the Update on Costs of Incarceration from the Office of the Parliamentary Budget Officer. (PBO, 2018) some costs are not included in this table 2-1. These costs include health care; trades and food services; transportation; expansion costs; time served for pre-sentence custody; correctional interventions and internal services; cultural programming and needs; community supervision such as regional treatment centres (psychiatric hospitals); private security (Commissionaires); Canada Border Services; Public Works and Government Services Canada. Other costs that are not specifically elaborated but may or may not appear in the "all other expenses." One percent may include clothing and footwear, hygiene, linens, seasonal clothing, internet and communication costs. These may appear as a minor cost, however, they are an expenditure regardless.

I question the transparency in this report, considering the "offender to staff" ratio is stated as "1.37:1," and the incarceration cost for one male inmate in minimum security is stated as $130 per day. For $130, the salary of the staff member may be included, but all the other costs per category are not. The 73% is derived from dividing 1/1.37 which amounts to 72.99%. Further the $130 per day is divided by 73% and by eight hours per day, which amounts to $11.86 per hour. The 73% of offender and staff ratio is calculated as the staff earning $11.86 per hour, which I suspect is false.

As mentioned earlier in this research, Kim Pate (2019) asserts that the majority of Indigenous women are kept in high security or segregation at a cost of $600,000 per year. The report from PBO indicates that the cost of high security/segregation is $463,045; however, it is also noted that only institution-specific costs are included, and that Ontario has only published figures regarding the number of inmates who are in segregation. Of the seven female penitentiaries in Canada, Ontario houses one only, which represents 14% of the total. I am suggesting that there may be a disproportion between the reported $463,045 and the $600,000 Kim Pate relates. The difference in these costs is just over 77%.

Meanwhile, community placement as a method of alternative justice in Canada is priced at $85,653 per year per person (Monkman 2018, CBC News). This is a substantial difference from the $343,810 per year per woman it currently costs in federal prison. The John Howard Society report the total budget for the prison system in Canada at $20 billion per year. This is based on the current (September 2019) number of inmates of 37,541; to multiply the inmate population by $85,653, the total would be $3.2 billion. For women only, the total would be $1,286,199,709 ($1.28 billion).

The methods explaining the manners of how the judiciary and the state may forecast the monetary allocations for incarceration as a means to satisfy the viability of the industries who supply the prison system could be as simple as averaging the total incarceration from year to year. Many employment sectors benefit from the allocations of incarceration, and many jobs would be adversely affected should the industry of incarceration decline.

According to the John Howard Society, of the other areas of federal spending in 2018, Aboriginal Affairs was $10 billion, the Department of Health was under $3 billion, Veteran Affairs was approximately $3.5 billion. Other yearly costs are elaborated in the article also. They report that correction/justice is one of the most expensive departments. The organization relates that "spending per capita on criminal justice went up by 23% while crime rates went down by 25%" (John Howard Society 2018). They also mirror my prior statements that billions of dollars per year could be reallocated, perhaps to alternative justice methods. "Much evidence shows that time in jail does not reduce crime and may actually result in more crime" (John Howard Society 2018).

4.2 FINDINGS, ANALYSIS, AND DISCUSSION

Who exactly is insisting on the over-incarceration of Indigenous women? This question remains to be answered. In the process of formulating closure, I envision a linear chain of reasoning. Each link is only as strong as the other; each link is a distinct entity, but the composition of all is what we define as a chain. The links at one end of the chain remain unaware of the stability (or instability) of the links further down, leaving the chain's success to chance.

In a fierce commitment to my truth, I helped my prior client navigate the world of law after she was charged in 2017 and before the law had taken a stronghold of the situation to wrongfully convict her. In that small community where Legal Aid was practically inaccessible—other than the infrequent visits to the community when the weather allowed it—I tapped my resources and questioned my allies by phone in order to formulate a strategy for this woman. Had this woman followed the predetermined steps of attending court and pleading guilty, the chances of her defending her innocence would likely be zero. The resources I questioned strongly encouraged a strategy immediately following her charge. Game theory insists that accessing a professional strategist to aid in formulating a new game plan falls within the rules of the game.

Critical theory, criminological theory, game theory, and the various evidence-based approaches used in the composition of this research, advocate for the use of strategic planning. Feminist theory takes a stance that all must gain from a process and potential outcome.

In a broad sense, strategic planning aids in formulating a "next choice," all the while maintaining credibility and acquiring "perfect knowledge." In my quest to minimize the negative outcome for the client mentioned above, the next choice was to access my allies (in this case I called Legal Aid in another town) to question them. I felt I acquired perfect knowledge from that conversation. In this client case, and in my methods as a social worker, the perfect knowledge was helpful in maintaining an absence of domination. In the presence of domination, her lawyer was steering her towards a plea of guilt, which was not fitting for her situation. The several alternatives that Dixit expresses involved the alternatives which were available to my client:; one was pleading guilty and feeling powerless to the decisions of the court, in essence, guilty by association. Other alternatives available to her were to provide her blood results to her lawyer and insist that it be used in her defence. She also provided her banking records, which were consistent with earning a regular salary. Therefore an absence of earnings from the sale of drugs. A lot of the work I accomplished with this client was through being assertive but not bold, being persistent in maintaining her innocence, insisting that her lawyer not follow the status quo. Strategic planning, in this sense, operates from the absence of domination, where a zero sum is not the objective of the proposed outcome. Dixit argues that "most strategic situations involve a longer sequence of decisions with several alternatives at each" (Dixit and Nalebuff 2010).

4.2 ASSUMPTIONS AND LIMITATIONS

There are many ways to withhold and distort information, some of which have been exemplified in this research project. This project is a limitation in itself, considering that numbers are reported improperly. While at times it may appear that the rate of incarceration is high, some agencies do not make a distinction between federal or provincial inmates; the monetary numbers reported by the Parliamentary Budget Officer (PBO) are federal, and the inmate population may incorporate all tiers of prisons. Rightfully so, agencies who advocate for incarcerated persons accomplish as much work for all tiers, therefore at the end of the fiscal year, a person is a person, and no distinction is made between which tier of government brought them to prison.

Limitations become apparent when the same story is reported in various mediums, but the numbers do not relate. Relying on the state's published documents does not always facilitate the tabulation either. The sociological phrase "The medium is the message" (McLuhan 1964) was coined by a Canadian communication theorist in his book *Understanding Media: The Extensions of Man*. Thus, the medium is rendered useful in deciphering the information. However assumptions cannot be formulated from those either.

From a legal perspective, it may be less effortful to abide by the modus operandi, but when compared to a social work or therapeutic method, the methodology cannot be explained in one sentence, nor a paragraph. Again, it would not be wise to formulate an assumption that a person is guilty based on modus operandi. There are hundreds of factors that contribute to the action itself, and its totality cannot be explained in a sentence either. If I can use the example of my client in a small Northern Ontario town, the woman was charged because she was in the presence of a drug dealer. Therefore, the modus operandi was guilt by association. From a social work perspective, the reasoning for this client was layered and complex. She needed a temporary place to live (so we engaged in conversation about her safety, her well-being, her future plans, and more). From the legal implications and from a social work approach the work involved self-confidence, anger, frustration, possible child welfare issues, the varied costs of defending herself, her self-worth, and so much more. But in the legal approach . . . she was guilty by association (modus operandi).

Flaws and uncertainties become evident when Johnson states that "the more we rely upon incarceration, the more we are forced to incarcerate" (Johnson 2019, 98) In some communities, and in the absence of funding, some courts have no choice but to incarcerate. Not every town or region has resources and services such as alternative justice or even counselling for complex histories and traumas. At the current time, one Gladue report takes an average of six months to prepare, considering the multitude of people and sources one must access and research to put a report together. In the absence of a Gladue report, the courts often don't have options other than to incarcerate in order to maintain some safety within communities.

While living in a small Northern Ontario community in 2016, I needed to access a government office to update a piece of identification. There was no permanent service of that type in the community, however, an official from another town had a prearranged schedule; he came to town once a month to serve the clients that had registered for a particular day. The first month that I had a scheduled appointment, the official announced on the day of that everything would be rescheduled for the following month. On that future date, the official announced that illness would prevent them from relocating two hours away to accomplish their work. Thereafter, no known schedule was communicated. In order to acquire the identification that I needed, I drove five hours to another, larger city to obtain it. It can be easy to make assumptions that all communities have access to services such as this. And it is also easy to make assumptions that agencies and government fulfill all of their obligations. In my case, perhaps I was the only registered client for the day, and that relocation to our community could not be warranted. However, making clients wait an extra two months for a required service is negligent. Many communities in Canada are underserviced, and for someone who is obligated to satisfy the courts, these restrictions are a reality.

Clark provides many examples of limitations that can be difficult, or impossible, to overcome: poverty, lack of education (education requiring money to undertake), racism, and the spectrum of social injustices and ills, systemic discrimination, marginalization, relocation, family commitments and obligations, victimization, colonialism and its numerous elements. These are a few of the topics Clark makes reference to in his report (2019).

One report I intended to cite in this research project was meant to serve as a tabulation of all prisons within a prescribed sphere. In reality, the report was missing six prisons that had not provided their statistics and tabulations. Such neglect prevents the public from obtaining and referencing correct information. I question whether the central office does not have an obligation to report accurately and in its entirety. Is the reported information deemed satisfactory for its intended purpose?

As a supposition in this chapter, a shift in power would be the outcome if more people accessed the alternate methods of restorative justice. As Chartrand suggests, not enough people access the alternative methods of justice. Without naming the organization, there is one in particular that provides for forty-nine First Nations communities. The expertise and commitment towards the wellbeing of people does exist.

While in university in 2011, I attended a lecture within the Faculty of Political Science. The professor stated that if all eligible Indigenous people voted for the same party, there exists a population large enough to win any election. Therefore if the Indigenous population accessed the legal intervention methods that are available at this time, the funding and the magnitude of services would have the potential of growing exponentially. At the moment, the public servants and the caretakers fall under the same umbrella as the funding body for the prisons (government). When the people deemed guilty make use of community justice centres, the regulators and caretakers would be the Indigenous people including Elders and administrators. Therefore the money would no longer be allotted to the public service sector, but to the Indigenous helping agencies who perform the tasks.

Funding is yet another limitation that is worthy of discussion. At the present time, the money is allocated entirely to the prison system. The money that would satisfy a restorative approach would, I assume, come from the same pocket. However, both methods of restitution cannot be satisfied within the limitations of the allotted money. The process of reallocation could very likely be achieved effectively, but we are limited, as the prisons are full and the money cannot be reallocated until incarceration rates subside. Both systems cannot be funded from the same money at the same time. The political agenda and triumphs could not be spoken with confidence if industry held firmly to the supposition proposed in this project: that prisons contribute to the profitability of industries that could not continue if the rate of incarceration were to decline. Furthermore, many employment sectors would be adversely affected.

Assuming the hearsay is accurate, and that the Indigenous population currently surpasses the growth rate amongst all other groups in Canada, an alternate method of restorative justice would provide the thousands upon thousands of Indigenous women in prison with the opportunity to vote and use their voices to promote and shape future leadership. The assumption is that mothers and women would draw upon the decades and centuries of injustices committed upon women to influence a certain shift in power.

The limitations and assumptions are many. The lived experiences of Indigenous women speak for themselves.

Chapter 5

5.1 TWO-EYED SEEING APPROACH AS A MORAL-JUDICIAL PARADIGM

In Norway, the federal criminal justice system is founded on restorative justice principles, along with the rehabilitation of inmates. According to Prison Insiders 2022 accessed on February 25, 2023, Norway reports having one of the lowest rates of recidivism in the world, with approximately 3,124 inmates as of 2022. With a population of 5,441,356, the offenders represent .0007% of the population. In Canada, the offender/population ratio is .001%.

The Norwegian model uses alternative penalties, also known as "penalties of society." Some of the tenets of the Norwegian model include obligations to work; community service measured in hours ranging from thirty to seventy to be completed within one year; regular meetings with officials; and abiding by an implementation plan drawn up by the correctional system under the framework of the court order; electronic monitoring devices to be worn on the ankle twenty-four hours a day. The drug-related crimes also follow an alternative to unconditional imprisonment, which follows a similar framework.

In Kenora, Ontario, the provincial government has formed a collaboration with Indigenous leadership and organizations, justice partners, and others, in order to establish the Kenora Justice Centre (Attorney General 2019). In 2016, almost 90% of individuals in the Kenora jail self-identified as Indigenous; these numbers depict an 18% increase from 2014 and 2017, while crime rates across the province are declining in frequency and severity (Attorney General 2019). Within this new model, the over-representation of Indigenous people in the local criminal justice system will be addressed through various initiatives that join law enforcement and the judiciary with community interventions. The announcement of this new model was made by the Ontario government in September 2019, and the pilot was launched in the winter of 2019/20. The advisory council is comprised of Indigenous leadership, judiciary and justice partners, community leaders, health and social service organizations, and housing providers who will inspire and advise the development of the centre. The Kenora Justice Centre pilot project forms part of a collaborative design process that will inform the establishment of comprehensive justice centres in other communities (Attorney General 2019). The model is designed to improve the outcomes for offenders, victims and communities using a holistic approach of accountability, while providing offenders with access to services that reduce the risk of reoffending. The commitment that is embodied by all parties is to promote collaboration and address risk factors while supporting the victims, the communities, and the offenders.

In the Kenora model specifically, parallel criminal and Indigenous restorative justice methods aim to augment referrals to cultural justice programs already in existence. The reduction of bail and remand populations, as well as the provision of multi-sectoral intervention, forms part of the aim as well. The Ministry of Attorney General continues to "explore pilot opportunities to increase the use of a diversion which include enhancing and encouraging the use of post-charge diversion; implementing a small-scale court outside of the conventional courthouse, co-located with culturally relevant, trauma-informed services that promote healing and wellness; improving discharge planning and reintegration supports; expanding opportunities to advocate for transitional and supportive housing; and partnerships with local Land-Based Healing and Wellness Program" (MGA Justice Centres, Nov 16, 2021).

Adam Kahane conceptualizes the creation of new realities in his book, *Power and Love* (2010), making use of "the drive to self-realization" (x) and "the drive to unity" (x) simultaneously. Kahane's work is to reframe social challenges around the world in order for organizations to benefit from alternative interpretations that may be viewed as oppositional. He explains the distinctions between "power" and "love" and describes how "these two fundamental drives generate social change." Herb Nabigon explains in *Indigenous Social Work Theory* (Turner, 1996, 18-36) that reviewing or looking twice is the concept as defined in the term introspection. It is through the action of looking twice that issues are seen from two different perspectives. The action of reviewing is also comprised in the "Two-Eyed Seeing" approach, which provides an opportunity to view and interpret something from a broader vantage point. The exploration of both methods of experiencing self-actualization abides by the proponents of "Two-Eyed Seeing," coined by Elder Albert Marshall (2004) as guiding principles for the realization of beneficial outcomes if multiple perspectives are considered. Two-eyed seeing can be understood in many ways. For one if a person incorporates two worldviews before arriving at a conclusion, they have made use correctly. For the purpose of this book two-eyed seeing is referenced in two different manners. For one as a moral-judicial solution where perpetrators can resolve their crime according to the tenets of the criminal code yet with the application of moral approaches or interventions. The second intended implication of two-eyed seeing in this book refers to what Kahane exemplifies as the use of neither aggressive nor submissive solutions. In essence in this book and in this context, it can be described as a method of achieving balance where the two factors are of equal relevance. The example of restorative justice in Norway and Kenora is making use of Two-Eyed Seeing—but is it enough?

When addressing over-representation of Indigenous women in prison is understood as a social change, certain descriptive words come to mind in the midst of the process of solution finding. These words can include resistance, aggression, imposition, defeat, hopelessness, and many more. The reported statistics in this work indicate that the situation is not improving. To reiterate Johnson, who stresses that "the more we rely upon incarceration, the more we are forced to incarcerate" (2019, 98), Kahane relates that in order to conceptualize new social realities, neither "aggressive war nor submissive peace" works. Instead, he describes "collective creation" as a solution to the toughest social challenges. He is guided by the work of Paul Tillich, theologian and philosopher who defines power as "the drive of everything living to realize itself" and love "as the drive to reconnect and make whole that which has become or appears fragmented." In terms of creating, Kahane expresses that the assumption of "an empty world: an open frontier . . . a blank canvas" is incorrect, just as "the doctrine of terra nullius" was incorrectly termed upon arrival to a new land in the 1700s. He stresses that in order to reconnect the fragments of a socially complex challenge, such as the practice of incarceration, the system must be viewed as a whole, where the diverse perspectives and interests, competing voices and ideas, purposefully come together to reconcile failures and successes. Kahane exemplifies such a "dynamic balance" as "walking on two legs." In this action, one leg is used at a time; they are not used together. The movement cannot be achieved with one leg only. He uses this example to show how one might "reconcile power and love in practice." In the context of the choices available between incarceration or alternative justice systems, each system remains aware of the abilities and fundamental principles of the other and allows for a fluid "co-creation of new social realities" (Kahane 2010).

Where Johnson expresses the need to "rely on incarceration," Kahane argues that "power-over abuses force and compulsion to suppress or oppress or dominate another" (2010). By power-over I explain a concept similar to the domination vs. dominated referred earlier in this book. In the example of non-consensual sterilization, the women who underwent the surgery are defined as dominated (action inflicted involuntarily) while the medical professionals and legislation who permitted such a procedure are deemed as dominators (performing non-consented surgery) at their will. When women experience powerlessness within the legal system, where their circumstances are not given consideration, they essentially feel dominated. In such instances, Kahane expresses that the "degenerative impacts of power-over are resolutely persistent" (Kahane 2010).

In the film *Kanyini,* the Australian Aboriginal leader Bob Randall expresses that the challenges for Indigenous people were borne from being "estranged from the four aspects of life that are essential to survival: their belief system or law, their land or country, their spirituality, and their families" (Kahane 2010). Randall asserts in the film that "the purpose of life is to be part of everything that is" (Kahane 2010). This is the opposite of the outcome of being incarcerated, yet it is the objective of restorative justice systems.

Paul Tillich's philosophical definition of love is "the drive towards the unity of the separated." In other words, power (the judiciary) and love can co-create in a manner that Kahane defines as "generative." In this context, a relationship between power and love is possible, utilizing the principle of unity where all perspectives and interests are addressed for a common objective (Kahane 2010). Kahane cites the psychologist Carl Jung: "only what is separated may be properly joined." However, he stresses that although co-creation between systems is achievable, "We must consciously and carefully observe both our power and our love, and neither confuse nor choose between nor forcibly fuse them."

The systems of judiciary and alternative justice are distinct phenomena and are not meant to be fused; however, by remaining mindful of each other, the combined force could be generative—as opposed to each being singularly degenerative.

Leadership is built on the premise that humans inherently possess confidence and trust from childhood. In *The Emergence of the Breath of Life Theory* (2011), Dr. Cindy Blackstock demonstrates that humans possess qualities of self-actualization at birth which is contrary to Maslow's belief that humans reach the pinnacle of self-actualization after a lifetime of small accomplishments within each tier of his described hierarchy. For these principles to hold up in the face of challenges in a lifetime, and in support of the inherent qualities stated above, women and children discussed in this chapter can further build on their leadership skills starting from birth. However, amidst incarceration (and recidivism) both women and children loose important qualities which they were born with.

When faced with the absence of a parent, the child is subjected to a series of setbacks. The physiological needs—such as shelter, sleep, clothing—may not be provided as they should be because of the environment the child is relocated to. The morality, family, and health that are found in the safety tier of Maslow's hierarchy also have the propensity to be absent or reduced. In the absence of these alone, a child's opportunity to ascend in the hierarchy of needs is greatly reduced. In the teachings of leadership from which confidence and trust are included, the child again experiences a sense of absence, which further diminishes or halts the attainment of self-actualization.

The relational worldview principle (Blackstock, Cross, 1997, 2007) takes into consideration that each quadrant is connected to all other quadrants at the centre of the circle. To explain the concept of quadrants, draw a circle and draw two lines from one side to the other (as if you were cutting a pie in four equal pieces). Each quadrant (each piece in the pie) is connected to all other pieces at the centre. In the Cree Medicine Wheel teachings (Nabigon, Turner, 1996), the centre is identified as the "hub," which represents each individual. The centre or "the self" is thus joined to all quadrants from birth and has access to all facets of the representations of each quadrant; most contribute to the development of leadership from the first breath of life. To further exemplify, the quadrant to the East can represent infancy (or the beginning of a something). I use this direction to interpret the beginning of a project which is new to me and I continue with the understanding that I am learning some new methods – not unlike a child who is learning new skills. The next quadrant is youth and encompasses the continued learning yet has gained skills to enhance their life. The third quadrant which faces West is adulthood where knowledge has been accumulated since infancy, but absolute knowledge does not exist. In the Northern quadrant is elderhood. At the centre of the circle each direction is connected – yet that absolute centre point is the hub (Nabigon) or the self. There exists much literature explaining the four quadrants also called the four directions and the teachings associated with them. My definition above is not the teaching a person would obtain from Elders but provided to exemplify the relationships that exist during all stages of life.

When this precept is applied to the context of the development of leadership from a breath of life model and starting from infancy, the family and community become foundational elements of growth and well-being; this encompasses the full spectrum of Maslow's tier entitled "safety." However, such a development must begin at the first breath of life.

The research accomplished by both Blackstock and Maslow derives from the teachings of the Blackfoot worldview, even if the conceptualization appears polarized from both researchers. Maslow's theory makes use of the accomplishments to date aiming for self-realization, essentially looking back and building upon the success achieved. If one does not have shelter, how can this person consider employment or productivity in their life? As a social worker, I always asked the client sitting in front of me if they had eaten that day. This provided me with insight into their ability to discuss their concerns. Maslow's theory uses a method of ascent that can only build on the prior accomplishments: in essence, looking back as a precursor to moving forward. This in itself can be conceptualized as a second viewing. Blackstock also builds her Two-Eyed Seeing approach, but from a perspective that the potential of self-actualization is inherent at birth and needs to be further enhanced possibly with the implementation of the community, family, and environment in order to contribute to the ascent to leadership. Blackstock relates that self-actualization is inherent for all humans, thus it is viewed as the foundation capable of upholding any structural accomplishment such as leadership, critical perspective, trust, and confidence. Self-actualization is thus defined as the ability to critically analyze situations in a holistic manner, encompassing the skills of introspection, spiritual attunement, and transcendence (Blackstock 2011).

It is proposed that the qualities that form leadership abilities may be developed at an early age. However, the attainment of leadership qualities—which encompass independent and critical thinking, confidence in self and environment—may be implausible for certain populations. I define the intents of these historical occurrences—such as residential schools and the removal of women from their communities—as elimination, whether their purpose is to eradicate culture, language, worldviews, knowledge, or otherwise.

Examples and statistics are presented in Chapter 4, indicating that alternate methods of justice are available, and that incarceration is not the only option. However, if alternate methods of remedial action are proven successful around the world, I question the motive for the increasing rate of Indigenous women in prison. It seems very clear that there are intentions of financial gain.

Johnson (2019) relates that the various parties involved in a case are not healing as a result of incarceration, and the rates of recidivism are rising rapidly for specific populations. The system must consider alternate methods.

Conclusion

WHEN I AMASS THE KEY words and phrases from the prior chapter—realize itself; reconnect; make whole; come together; reconcile; unity; essential to survival; purpose of life; be part of; and contribute to development—it becomes clear that people already possess the methods synonymous to those phrases, which include regenerate; revitalize; alliance; and integrity. It is conceivable to maintain a system where families are not divided. Norway has implemented that concept, and their rate of recidivism and crime remains low compared to Canada. A system of restorative justice is slowly being implemented in Canada, but sometimes the process of change feels too slow.

In reading various literature. The assumption is that courts that have a high number of cases involving Indigenous people are recognized as Gladue courts, but that is not the case (Clark, 32). Many courthouses lack the expertise of trained professionals with relevant backgrounds—such as resident Gladue writers and Indigenous court workers who can connect the accused to the appropriate resources—and access to community-based justice programs.

It is conceivable for communities and restorative justice programs to be available not only to the accused but also for the family members. It would not be uncommon for all family members to be affected by the legal issue, and by the same token it is common for the family members to be negatively impacted by the absence of the accused. When I use the synonymous words of "alliance," "unity," and "come together," I am understanding that the family would have the opportunity to heal and understand as an alliance.

When I assert and expand upon the concepts of Dr. Blackstock that children have the inherent understanding of leadership qualities, I am stating that a child could have an important role in participating in their parent's progress. Offenders in cities and regions that do not have community justice programs or restorative programs in close proximity may benefit from having their children and loved ones with them. Not only would the children maintain their sense of security with their parent or family member, they would have an opportunity to learn from the process. In an equal manner, the parent would have the assurance that their children are safe and have access to the necessities.

Randall asserts the four aspects that are essential to survival and emphasizes that people have a need to be connected "to everything that is"; this includes family, environment, which is described earlier as a "fit," to which I add spiritual freedom, nurturance, guidance and support.

Although the rise of restorative justice is forthcoming, is it enough? If the assertion that the budget for justice is $20 billion and 50% are Indigenous women in some prisons, it would justify a larger allocation of money to restorative centres.

If the research about leadership and inherent knowledge from birth is correct, it would follow to suggest asking offenders what their healing journey would look like. People know their truth in the same way they know the solution: people know what they need. Programs can be implemented based on the suggested methods, encompassing twofold solutions as opposed to a singularly degenerative system.

At the current time, the system of incarceration is changing, but resistance to a generative solution is still apparent, making the reliance on incarceration necessary. When an alliance and/or a two-eyed approach can be cemented in the foundational principles of prevention and healing, the fragments of a broken system will begin to resemble a collective creation.

References

Alfred, Taiaiake, Gerald. 2005. *Wasáse: indigenous pathways of action and freedom*. Toronto, Ontario:Broadview Press, Ltd.

Anderson, Kim. 2000. *A Recognition of Being Reconstructing Native Womanhood: The Dismantling of Gender Equity*. Toronto, Ontario: Sumach Press.

Anderson, Barry and Dawn Anderson. 2009. *Manufacturing Guilt: Wrongful Convictions in Canada*. Halifax and Winnipeg, Canada: Fernwood Publishing.

Arendt, Hannah. 1998. *The Human Condition*. Chicago, London: University of Chicago Press, Ltd.

Attorney General. 2019. "Ontario Taking Next Steps to Establish Kenora Justice Centre. Government working with Indigenous community partners to enhance community safety." Accessed September 26 2019. https://news.ontario.ca/en/release/53942/ontario-taking-next-steps-to-establish-kenora-justice-centre

Banda, Andrew. 2019. *A Study of Multiple Causes of Recidivism*. Beau Bassin, Mauritius: Lap Lambert Academic Publishing.

Baron-Cohen, Simon. 2012. *The Science of Evil: on Empathy and the Origins of Cruelty*. New York, NY: Basic Books, A Member of the Perseus Books Group.

Bereska, Tami Marie. M. 2018. *Deviance, Conformity, and Social Control in Canada.*
5th edition. North York, Ontario: Pearson Canada Inc.

Bickenbach, Jerome. E. and Jaqueline M. Davies. 1997. *Good reasons for better arguments: an introduction to the skills and values of critical thinking.* Peterborough, Ontario, Orchard Park, NY, Hadleigh, Essex, England, Rozelle, NSW: Broadview Press Ltd.

Blackburn, Mark. 2019. "It's disappointing: Corrections maintains status quo as number of Indigenous women tops 40% of prison population." National News, Canada.

Blackstock, Cindy. 2011. "The Emergence of the Breath of Life Theory." Journal of Social Work Values and Ethics. White Hat Communications. https://fncaringsociety.com/publications/emergence-breath-life-theory

Braithwaite, John. 2002. *Restorative Justice and Responsive Regulation.* New York, NY: Oxford University Press.

Carter, Sarah. 1999. *Aboriginal People and Colonizers of Western Canada to 1900.*
Toronto, ON: University of Toronto Press Inc.

Chartrand, Vicki. 2018. "Broken System: Why is a quarter of Canada's prison population Indigenous." British Columbia: The Tyee.

Chilisa, Bagele. 2012. *Indigenous Research Methodologies.* London, UK: Sage Publications Ltd.

Clark, Scott. 2019, 31. "Over-representation of Indigenous People in the Canadian Criminal Justice System: Causes and Responses." Department of Justice Canada: Research and Statistics Division.

Comack, Elizabeth and Gillian Balfour. 2004. *The Power to Criminalize: Violence, Inequality and the Law.* Halifax, NS: Fernwood Publishing.

Cote-Meek, Sheila. 2014. *Colonized Classrooms: Racism, Trauma and Resistance in Post-Secondary Education.* Black Point, Nova Scotia: Fernwood Publishing.

Cragg, Wesley and Christine Koggel. 2005. Contemporary Moral Issues. Toronto, Canada: McGraw-Hill Ryerson.

Cross, Terry. L. 1997. "Relational Worldview Model." https://www.sprc.org › files › resource-program

Dixit, Avinash.K. and Barry J. Nalebuff. 1991. *Thinking Strategically: The Competitive Edge in Business, Politics, and Everyday Life.* New York, USA: W.W. Norton & Company, Inc.

Dixit, Avinash. K. and Barry. J. Nalebuff. 2010. *The Art of Strategy: A Game Theorist's Guide to Success in Business and Life.* New York, NY, London: W.W. Norton & Company, Inc.

Echo-Hawk, Walter. R. 2013. *In the Light of Justice: The Rise of Human Rights in Native America and UN Declaration on the Rights of Indigenous Peoples.* Golden, CO: Fulcrum Publishing.

Elizabeth Fry Society. 2021. https://caefs.ca/projects-and-initiatives/

Epp, Daniel. 2015. "The Consequences of Error in Criminal Justice." *Harvard Law Review.* Vol. 128, Number 4.

Flanagan, Thomas. 2008. *First Nations? Second Thoughts.* Montreal, Québec, Kingston, Ontario. London, Ithaca. McGill-Queen's University Press

Garland, David. 2002. *The Culture of Control Crime and Social Order in Contemporary Society.* Chicago, USA: The University of Chicago Press; Oxford University Press.

Gehl, Lynn. 2017. *Claiming Anishinaabe, Decolonizing the Human Spirit.* Regina, Saskatchewan: University of Regina Press

Gitterman. Alex. 1996. "Advances in the life: model of social work practice." Social Work Treatment, 4th Edition. New York, NY: The Free Press.

Government of Canada. 2017. http://www.justice.gc.ca/eng/cj-jp/tcjs-tsjp/about-ausujet.html.

Grant, Agnes. 2009. "Feminism and Aboriginal Culture: One Woman's View." *First Voices*: An Aboriginal Women's Reader. Toronto, ON: Inanna Publications and Education Inc.

Green, Joyce (ed.). 2017. *Making Space for Indigenous Feminism.* Winnipeg, Manitoba, Black Point, Nova Scotia: Fernwood Publishing.

Hamilton, Alvin. Associate Chief Justice. 1991. Report of the Aboriginal Justice Inquiry of Manitoba. http://www.ajic.mb.ca/volumel/toc.html

Hargreaves, Allison. 2017. *Violence Against Indigenous Women: Literature, Activism, Resistance.* Waterloo, Ontario: Wilfred Laurier University Press.

Health Canada. 2020. https://www.canada.ca/en/services/health/determinants-health.html

Heinonen, Tuula and Len Spearman. 2010. *Social Work Practice: Problem Solving and Beyond* (3rd edition). Toronto, ON: Nelson Education Ltd.

John Howard Society. 2018. "Financial facts on Canadian prisons." John Howard Society of Canada. Accessed August 23, 2019. https://johnhoward.ca/blog/financial-facts-canadian-prisons/

Johnson, Harold R. 2019. *Peace and Good Order*. Toronto, Ontario: Penguin Random House, McClelland and Stewart.

Johnson, Harold R. 2016. *Firewater: How Alcohol is Killing My People (And Yours)*.
Regina, SK: University of Regina Press.

Justice Canada. 2018. https://www.justice.gc.ca/eng/rp-pr/jr/jf-pf/2018/march01.html

Kahane, Adam M. 2010. *Power and Love: A Theory and Practice of Social Change*.
Oakland, CA: Berrett-Koehler Publishers, Inc.

Kaiser-Derrick, Elspeth. 2019. *Implicating the System: Judicial Discourses in the Sentencing of Indigenous Women*.
Winnipeg, Manitoba: University of Manitoba Press.

Katlatont Gabriel-Doxtater, Brenda and Arlette Kawanatatie Van den Hende. 1995. *At The Wood's Edge: An Anthology of the History of the People of Kanehsatà:ke*.
Kanesatake, Québec: Kanesatake Education Centre.

Kovach, Margaret. 2010. *Indigenous Methodologies: Characteristics, Conversations, and Context*. Toronto, Ontario: University of Toronto Press.

Lee, Judith A.B. 1996. "The empowerment approach to social work practice." Social Work Treatment (Fourth Edition). New York, NY: The Free Press.

LeFrançois, Brenda A., Robert Menzies, Geoffrey Reaume (editors). 2013. Mad Matters: A Critical Reader in

Canadian Mad Studies. Toronto, Ontario: Canadian Scholars' Press Inc.

Maidment, MaDonna. 2009. *When Justice is a Game: Unravelling Wrongful Convictions in Canada.* Halifax and Winnipeg, Canada: Fernwood Publishing.

Mannette, Joy (editor). 1992. *Elusive Justice: Beyond the Marshall Inquiry.* Halifax, Nova Scotia: Fernwood Publishing.

Maslow, Abraham H. 1999. *Toward a Psychology of Being.* New York, Chichester, Weinheim, Brisbane, Singapore, Toronto: John Wiley & Sons, Inc.

McGillivray, Anne and Brenda Comaskey. 1999. *Black Eyes All the Time; The Historical Context.* Toronto, Ontario: University of Toronto Press.

McGregor, Deborah and Jean-Paul Restoule, Rochelle, Johnston (editors). 2018. *Indigenous Research: Theories, Practices, and Relationships.* Toronto, Ontario: Canadian Scholars, imprint of CSP Books Inc.

Menzies, Heather. 2005. *The Seedlings Mattered: Teaching as Activism Equity meets Environmentalism.* Montreal, QC: McGill-Queen's University Press.

Mill, John Stuart. 2006. On Liberty and The Subjection of Women. London, England: Penguin Classic, Penguin Group.

Miller, Donald L. *Recidivism: Symptoms of a flawed criminal justice system.* Bolton, On. Manufactured by Amazon.ca. ISBN 9781699060186 provided in the absence of a publication date and page numbers within.

Ministry of the Attorney General (MAG). 2021. "Ontario's Justice Centre Pilots: An Innovative Community-Driven Justice Model for the Future."

Moreton-Robinson, Aileen (editor). 2016. *Critical Indigenous Studies: Engagements in First World Locations.* Tucson, Arizona: University of Arizona Press.

Mullaly, Bob. 2007. *The New Structural Social Work* (3rd edition). Don Mills, Ontario: Oxford University Press.

Nabigon, Herb and Ann Marie Mawhiney. 1996. "Aboriginal Theory: A Cree medicine wheel guide for healing first nations." Social Work Treatment, 4th edition. New York, NY: The Free Press

Nash, Marie and Robyn, Munford, Kieran O'Donoghue (editors). 2009. *Social Work Theories in Action.* London, UK and Philadelphia PA.: Jessica Kingsley Publishers.

Olsen Harper, Anita. 2009. "Is Canada Peaceful and Safe for Aboriginal Women?" *First Voices*: An Aboriginal Women's Reader. Toronto, ON: Inanna Publications and Education, Inc.

Parliamentary Budget Officer. 2018. https://www.pbo-dpb.gc.ca/en/

Parrott, Zach. "Gladue Case," in *The Canadian Encyclopedia.* 2017. https://www.thecanadianencyclopedia.ca/en/article/r-v-gladue

Perry, Barbara. 2008. *Silent Victims: Hate Crimes Against Native Americans.*
Tucson, Arizona: University of Arizona Press.

Prison Insiders 2022 https://www.prison-insider.com/en/countryprofile/norvege-2022

Rope, Olivia. 2013. "Protecting the rights of women offenders: A Job for the CEDAW Committee?" Accessed August 19, 2013. https://opcedaw.wordpress.com/2013/08/19/protecting-the-rights-of-women-offenders/

Rowe. William. 1996. "Client-Centered Theory: A person-centered approach." Social Work Treatment, 4th Edition. New York, NY: The Free Press.

Satzewich, Vick. 2011. *Issues in Canada: Racism in Canada*. Don Mills, Ontario: Oxford University Press.

Sinclair, Murray, Associate Chief Judge of the Provincial Court. 1991. "Report of the Aboriginal Justice Inquiry of Manitoba." http://www.ajic.mb.ca/volume.html

St-Amand, Nérée and Eugène LeBlanc. 2013. "Women in the 19th-Century Asylums: Three Exemplary Women," "A New Brunswick Hero." Mad Matters, A Critical Reader in Canadian Mad Studies. Toronto, ON: Canadian Scholars' Press Inc.

Statistics Canada. (2021) Retrieved from https://www.statcan.gc.ca/en/start

Tuhiwai Smith, Linda. 2008. *Decolonizing Methodologies: Research and Indigenous Peoples*. New York: Palgrave, Division of St Martin's Press, LLC.

Turner, Annie. Susan, Crompton, Stephanie, Langlois. 2013. « Aboriginal peoples in Canada: First Nations people, Métis and Inuit: National Household Survey 2011." Statistics Canada. https://www150.statcan.gc.ca/n1/daily-quotidien/130508/dq130508a-eng.html

Turner, Francis J (editor). 1979. Social Work Treatment: Interlocking Theoretical Approaches. New York, NY: The Free Press.

United Nations Human Rights, Office of the High Commissioner. 2019. Committee on the Elimination of Discrimination Against Women. https://www.ohchr.org/EN/HRBodies/CEDAW/Pages/CEDAWIndex.aspx

United Nations General Assembly (UNGA). 2010. "Rules for the Treatment of Women Prisoners and Non-Custodial Measures for Women Offenders (the Bangkok Rules)". United Nations Office on Drugs and Crime. A/C, 3, 65. https://www.unodc.org/documents/justice-and-prison-reform/Bangkok_Rules_ENG_22032015.pdf

Ury, William L., Jeanne M. Brett, Stephen B. Goldberg. 1993. "Getting Disputes Resolved: Designing Systems to Cut the Cost of Conflict." Cambridge, Mass: PON Books Program on Negotiation at Harvard Law School.

Valentich, Mary. 1996. "Feminist theory and social work practice." Social Work Treatment, 4th edition. New York, NY: The Free Press.

Wesley-Esquimaux, Cynthia C. 2009. "Trauma to Resilience: Notes on Decolonization." *Restoring the Balance: First Nations Women, Community, and Culture.* Winnipeg, Manitoba: University of Manitoba Press.

Wesley, Mandy. 2012. "Marginalized: The Aboriginal women's experience in federal corrections." Ottawa, ON: Public Safety Canada. https://www.publicsafety.gc.ca/cnt/rsrcs/pblctns/mrgnlzd/index-en.aspx

Williams III, Frank P. and Marilyn D. McShane. 1999. Criminological Theory, 3rd edition. Upper Saddle River, New Jersey: Prentice-Hall, Inc.

About the Author

ANNETTE VERMETTE lives in Sudbury, Ontario but has relocated several times to offer her social work expertise to other communities in Northern Ontario. Annette completed her Bachelor of Social Work and a Bachelor of Arts with Specialization in Indigenous Studies in Sudbury, and she is proud to have completed her studies as a mature student.

The varied populations she has encountered during her career have opened her eyes to the deficiencies in a moral-judicial approach towards the Indigenous women that are entwined with the law in underserviced communities. Annette's Métis heritage informs her understanding of moral issues faced by racialized populations, which in turn fuels her resolve to write about a controversial and crucial topic. Many have attempted to silence her voice, but she persists, out of determination to shed light on (these issues) and hope to inspire change.

She lives with her husband, Byron, and two cats, Chilli and Missy (short for Mischievous). She enjoys sewing, quilting, and cooking. Her adult children live nearby, and her grandchildren are her pride and joy.

Printed in the USA
CPSIA information can be obtained
at www.ICGtesting.com
LVHW090620091123
763425LV00001B/68